LEADING
WOMEN

Philanthropist
and Education
Advocate

# Melinda Gates

## CATHLEEN SMALL

Cavendish
Square

New York

Library of Congress Cataloging-in-Publication Data

Names: Small, Cathleen.
Title: Melinda Gates / Cathleen Small.
Description: New York : Cavendish Square, 2018. | Series: Leading women | Includes index.
Identifiers: ISBN 9781502627070 (library bound) | ISBN 9781502627087 (ebook)
Subjects: LCSH: Gates, Melinda, 1964---Juvenile literature. | Bill & Melinda Gates Foundation--History--Juvenile literature. | Women philanthropists--United States--Biography--Juvenile literature. | Humanitarianism--United States--Juvenile literature.
Classification: LCC HV28.G326 S63 2018 | DDC 361.7'632092--dc23

Editorial Director: David McNamara
Editor: Tracey Maciejewski
Copy Editor: Nathan Heidelberger
Associate Art Director: Amy Greenan
Designer: Lindsey Auten
Production Coordinator: Karol Szymczuk
Photo Research: J8 Media

# CONTENTS

## CHAPTER ONE

# Growing Up Melinda Gates

**M**elinda Gates's name is recognized worldwide, but not because of **ostentatious** celebrity. She's not a well-known actress or an award-winning singer, and she's not a regular on the celebrity club circuit. Rather, her name is recognized because she has spent the last couple of decades quietly but persistently dedicating her life to improving the lives of others. The fact that she's married to one of the

Melinda Gates, photographed here in 2015, was born Melinda Ann French.

world's richest men, multibillionaire Microsoft mogul Bill Gates, has afforded her the opportunity to be able to help people, but it's her own quiet determination that has been the real driving force behind the female half of the Bill and Melinda Gates Foundation.

## A Texas Schoolgirl

Before she was Melinda Gates, she was Melinda Ann French, born in Dallas, Texas, on August 15, 1964. This was the era of the Kennedy assassination, which put Dallas on the map in a tragic way. However Melinda's childhood was anything but tragic. Her father Raymond Joseph French, Jr., was an aerospace engineer in Dallas, and her mother, Elaine Agnes Amerland, stayed home to raise Melinda and her three siblings.

Melinda was Raymond and Elaine's second daughter. She has a sister, Susan, who is fourteen months older than her, and two younger brothers, Raymond and Steven. The four children helped out with the family's second income stream. In addition to her father's income from his job as an aerospace engineer, the family managed rental properties to bring in extra money. Melinda remembers her work at the properties: "I mowed lawns, I cleaned ovens—believe me, I did it all."[1] She even helped out with the financial end of things: "We would help him run the business and keep the books. We saw money coming in and money going out."[2] This attention to financial details was an early predictor of Melinda's pivotal role in the charitable foundations run by the Gates family.

Raymond and Elaine's dual income stream allowed the family to enjoy a middle-class life in Texas and helped them work toward their goal of sending all four of their children to college. Elaine regretted that she had not gone to college herself, and she intended for all of her children to take advantage of their opportunity to go. Education was a focus in their home, so it's not surprising that in her philanthropic work now, Melinda Gates is focused on education as a major part of her goals.

In the early 1980s, the French family managed the financial aspect of their rental properties using an Apple III computer, an amusing irony given that Melinda went on to marry the cofounder of Microsoft, Apple's largest competitor! It's somewhat surprising that the French family was using an Apple, given that by the mid-1980s, IBM and other **clones** (running Microsoft's operating system on their machines) *far* outnumbered Apple in sales—by 1985, PCs running the Microsoft OS dominated with nearly a 50 percent market share, compared to Apple's roughly 12 percent. But that early Apple III was part of what sparked Melinda's interest in computing.

The French family were Roman Catholics, and Melinda went to St. Monica Catholic School—part of St. Monica Catholic Church in Dallas, which she attended with her family. Melinda was a top student in elementary school, and her favorite subject was math.

Although most parents didn't encourage their daughters to pursue **STEM** subjects such as math in the late 1960s and early 1970s, Melinda's parents were very encouraging of their bright daughter, telling her, "You can get what you want."[3]

After graduating from St. Monica, Melinda went on to Ursuline Academy of Dallas, an all-girls Catholic high school in Dallas that was founded nearly 150 years ago. Melinda's interest in STEM subjects continued at Ursuline, where she continued her math studies and expanded into computers as well. These were the early days of personal computing, and Melinda was known for helping her fellow students learn how to program. Her math and computer teacher at Ursuline, Susan Bauer, commented, "She was hard-working and personable. She was one of the best students I ever had."[4] Bauer also remembers that "every day [Melinda] had a goal."[5]

Melinda claims those goals ranged from learning a new word to running a mile, but she admits that one goal was to be valedictorian, because she wanted to be admitted to an elite school, such as Notre Dame.

But Melinda wasn't all serious and studying. She was also captain of the drill team, volunteered as a **candy striper** at the hospital, and tutored at a school for less fortunate students.

Melinda was reportedly well liked at school. Susan Bauer remembers her as "never abrasive … She was always lovely and charming, and she would win people over by

Melinda Gates (*center*) with classmates at Ursuline Academy of Dallas

being persuasive."[6] Friends of the French family are tight lipped about Melinda's early years, respecting the French family's wish to respect Melinda's privacy. By all accounts, though, Melinda was a well-rounded student. Certainly her academic record was impressive—she was Ursuline's valedictorian for the graduating class of 1982, fulfilling the goal she had set for herself.

Melinda clearly has fond memories of her time at Ursuline—she has been an adviser and donor to the academy for decades. In 2006 and 2007, the Bill and Melinda Gates Foundation recognized the school by giving it two grants (one for $5 million and one for $2 million) to help build a new STEM center and fund STEM education at the school. Fittingly, the new STEM center is known as the French Family Science, Math, and Technology Center, and it was dedicated in 2010. In her speech at the dedication ceremony, Melinda said, "Since I graduated from Ursuline, I have been passionate about getting girls and women involved in science, math and technology. My vision is for this building to be an equalizer in the sciences. That is what my Ursuline education was for me."[7]

The French Family Center is certainly a large step forward in Melinda's vision for the school—it has ten science labs, nine math classrooms and a math lab, nine world-language classrooms, and three computer-science classrooms. Given the overarching interests of the Bill and Melinda Gates Foundation, the French Family Center's focus isn't surprising.

## College Days

Melinda left Texas in 1982, after graduating at the top of her class from Ursuline Academy. She moved to Durham, North Carolina, to attend Duke University, which was known for its strong computer-science department. Melinda had dreamed of attending Notre Dame, and indeed she was accepted at the prestigious school. During a campus visit, however, university officials told Melinda that they planned to shrink their computer-science department because computers were a "fad," so Melinda changed course and accepted a spot at Duke University.

The drive that had led Melinda to succeed at both St. Monica and Ursuline Academy and the work ethic that she had developed while helping out with her family's rental properties served her well at Duke. In a span of four years, she earned two bachelor's degrees: one in computer science and one in economics. She added on one more year at Duke to earn her MBA at their business school, the Fuqua School of Business.

Computer science wasn't a particularly common major for a woman at that time. Even now, statistics from the National Science Board indicate that women receive only 17.9 percent of bachelor's degrees awarded in computer science. When Melinda was studying computer science at Duke, the numbers were a little better, though men clearly still dominated the major. At the time, just over 35 percent of computer-science degrees were being earned by women, according to statistics compiled by the National Center for Education Statistics. In spite of this gender gap, Melinda felt comfortable in her department at Duke. She recalls of her undergraduate years:

> I was one of the few female computer science majors, back at a time when nobody was talking about women in STEM fields—but I never felt out of place at Duke. There was just no stigma attached to what I was doing, either inside or outside the department. I learned to work with male colleagues with many different styles and found I really enjoyed managing teams. As a result, I was confident enough to go on to become one of the few female leaders at Microsoft in its early days. During my time at Duke I learned how it felt to be supported as a young woman with big ideas.[8]

While at Duke, Melinda was a well-rounded student, much like she was at Ursuline. She led campus tours for prospective students, served on the freshman advisory council, and was a member of the Kappa Alpha Theta sorority. While she attended typical college parties and was sociable at them, she was also known for being fairly quiet. A former dorm-mate and sorority sister, Susan Lee

# Women in Computer Science

Like many STEM fields, computer science has always been a male-dominated field. However, female participation in the field experienced a long period of growth before beginning to decline again.

The National Center for Education Statistics compiled statistics for a forty-year period running from 1970 to 2011, and the results are somewhat surprising. The percentage of females earning a bachelor's degree in computer science in 1970 was predictably low: 13.6 percent. That began to rise by 1972, and it continued to rise until 1984, when it peaked at 37.1 percent. Then it began a steady decline, and in the last year of the study, 2010–2011, the percentage of women earning bachelor's degrees in computer science was 17.6 percent, almost as dismally low as where it had started.

There is no definitive answer as to why the percentage of women earning computer-science degrees rose and then declined again. Some cite societal pressures and attitudes, saying that women are still expected to pursue more traditionally female fields of work. But that doesn't explain the increase from the early 1970s to the mid-1980s. Some say it has to do with a change in the computer-science market—many IT and tech jobs are now being outsourced to overseas companies. But if that were the case, a similar downward trend should be seen in the number of men earning computer-science degrees, and that number has stayed relatively stable, with minor fluctuations over the years but no consistent downward trend.

There may be no answer, but there are movements trying to change this trend.

View of the French Family Science Center at Duke University

Greenfield, says of Melinda, "She lived in my dorm, she was in my sorority and I didn't know her very well."[9]

Other sorority sisters and dorm-mates remember Melinda as being hardworking and not terribly showy. She dressed relatively conservatively for a college student, with her hair pulled back simply in barrettes. She was also known at Duke for her monogamous dating—she didn't date many men, preferring to have longer-term relationships with fewer men rather than playing the field.

Much like Melinda recalls favorably her time at Ursuline Academy, she has similarly warm feelings about her time at Duke, calling it "some of the best years of my life"[10] and declaring "I loved my time at Duke."[11] She was elected to the university's board of trustees in 1996 (serving until 2003), and in 1998 the Bill and Melinda Gates Foundation gifted a $20 million **endowment**, one of the largest in the university's history, to launch a program designed to expand interdisciplinary teaching and research. The program, named the University Scholars Program, has a principal goal of identifying intellectually gifted students and providing them with the resources and forums to work together in unique, creative collaborations.

In 2002, just a few years before awarding a grant to Ursuline Academy for the construction of the French Family Center, the Bill and Melinda Gates Foundation made a similar grant to Duke, gifting $35 million toward the French Family Science Center, a 280,000-square-foot (26,000-square-meter) state-of-the-art research center for chemistry and biology laboratories.

A few years later, in 2007, the Bill and Melinda Gates Foundation joined the Duke Endowment and launched Duke Engage with a $30 million endowment. Duke Engage is a summer program that pairs Duke students with **nonprofits** or **nongovernmental organizations (NGOs)** to participate in civic engagement projects, such as environmental advocacy, community outreach, global health, education, and social justice. That same year, the foundation donated an additional $10 million to Duke to be awarded in financial aid to undergraduate and business school students.

The Duke Engage endowment was particularly important to Melinda because she recognizes that one thing missing from her years at Duke was a global awareness:

> When I was at Duke, my peers and I weren't very aware of the rest of the world. I knew there was a famine in Ethiopia, for example, but I thought it was a far-away problem that didn't really concern me. I wish I'd understood earlier how much there is to be gained from seeing the world in different ways ... The more you learn about different kinds of people and situations, the more you'll feel compelled to do something, and the richer your own life will be.[12]

In 2015, the Bill and Melinda Gates Foundation once again recognized Duke University, this time with a $20 million grant to the Duke Global Health Institute, intended to bolster worldwide research capacity to address global health challenges that Melinda and Bill Gates have recognized in their global travels for their philanthropic work.

The basic belief behind the Bill and Melinda Gates Foundation is that every life has equal value. As part of their attempt to lessen the inequities that exist between people worldwide, Melinda and Bill Gates have made global health and development a major focus of their foundation. They hope their donations and endowments to Duke, Melinda's **alma mater,** will further their efforts toward achieving this goal.

After five years at Duke, earning two bachelor's degrees and an MBA, it was time for Melinda to move on to the first step in her career: Microsoft.

# CHAPTER TWO

# *Working Her Way Up at Microsoft*

M elinda Gates is known for being incredibly smart. Indeed, multibillionaire businessman and philanthropist Warren Buffett famously said, "[Bill Gates is] smart as hell, obviously. But in terms of seeing the whole picture, [Melinda is] smarter."[1] Smarter than a man known for being one of the most brilliant tech minds of the twentieth and twenty-first centuries? A man who was

Melinda Gates at a speaking engagement in 2015

a National Merit Scholar and earned near-perfect scores on the SAT? That's no small compliment.

In terms of academic success, Melinda outperforms her famous husband, who dropped out of Harvard University to start Microsoft. Although Bill Gates later earned an honorary degree from Harvard, it's no match for his wife's three degrees from Duke.

Melinda's intelligence and academic success alone didn't lead her to become the incredibly wealthy and powerful philanthropist she is now. Without Microsoft, Melinda Gates might never have become a household name.

## Leaving the East for the West

While at Duke, Melinda had done a summer internship for IBM, and a recruiter from there had a helpful bit of advice when Melinda mentioned she had an interview with a new company coming up: "I told the recruiter that I had one more interview—at this young company, Microsoft. She said to me, 'If you get a job offer from them, take it, because the chance for advancement there is terrific.'"[2]

Melinda took the recruiter's advice and accepted a position at Microsoft, headquartered in the Seattle, Washington, area. In 1987, at just twenty-two years old, Melinda started in a marketing manager position for a software program that was a predecessor to Word, one of Microsoft's most successful and enduring products.

Ten people with MBAs had been recruited, and Melinda was the youngest of them and the only female, but she didn't mind. She had already been in a minority while completing her degree in the male-dominated computer-science department at Duke, and it didn't bother her. She saw her new colleagues as "a lot of idiosyncratic people. They were all so smart, and they were changing the world."[3]

However, Melinda was a bit taken aback by the corporate culture at Microsoft. At the top levels of the company, cofounder and CEO Bill Gates and business manager Steve Ballmer were known for being pretty tough on mid-level managers. Melinda recalls it as "a very **acerbic** company."[4] That acerbic attitude and culture were tough for Melinda to stomach, and she debated leaving the company.

Ultimately, though, she decided to stay. Four months after starting with the company in Seattle, Melinda accompanied Bill Gates and other employees to New York City for a PC Expo trade show, and at a group dinner in which she was seated next to the supposedly abrasive cofounder, she was surprised to find him funnier than she had expected.

## An Office Romance

Melinda Gates is such a strong, capable, successful woman in her charitable and philanthropic career that one might think it pointless to devote much space to the man in her life. But in the case of Melinda Gates, she and her husband, Bill, are a seamless, dedicated power team, each forming half of the incredibly successful Bill and Melinda Gates Foundation. In fact, Bill has stated as much, saying, "In my parents I saw a model where they were really always communicating, doing things together. They were really kind of a team. I wanted some of that magic myself."[5] So it's important to recognize how that team was formed.

Bill and Melinda Gates enjoyed sitting next to each other at that PC Expo dinner, where Melinda discovered Bill's sense of humor and Bill remembers being attracted to her looks. Over the years, Bill's love and dedication to Melinda has expanded far beyond a physical attraction, but on that first substantial meeting, he remembers finding her very attractive. Later, when asked what led him to want to marry Melinda, Bill said, "There's some magic there that's hard to describe."[6]

That same fall, the two ran into each other in the Microsoft parking lot on a Saturday afternoon—not unusual, since many of the early Microsoft employees worked weekends as they built the fledgling company. The two chatted a bit, and Bill asked Melinda for a date two weeks in the future. Melinda remembers saying, "Two weeks from Friday? That's not nearly spontaneous enough for me. I don't know. Call me up closer to the day."[7] Bill didn't wait until closer to the day—he waited just a few hours and then called and asked her to meet him later that very night.

For her part, Melinda was wary. Her billionaire boss had just asked her out, and while she liked his sense of humor, she had serious reservations about dating the boss. She had confided in her mother, who agreed that it was a bad idea for Melinda to date the CEO. So hesitant was Melinda that Bill remembers her as being "hard to get."[8]

But neither could deny the connection they shared. Melinda eventually relented, largely because Bill reminded her of her friends in the computer-science program back at Duke. In a 2015 *Forbes* interview (one of very few she has given), Melinda said, "When I look back, Bill was the same kind of guy I was hanging out with in college. I had a lot of respect for them, and they had respect for me. I was definitely attracted to his brilliant mind, but beyond that, his curiosity. And he has a huge sense of fun. I love that wry side of him."[9]

They ended up having their first date at Bill's house, because it was so late at night that they weren't sure what was open. Melinda had wanted spontaneity, and Bill had delivered by asking her for a date that very night—but it had to be after a computer user group meeting he was speaking at. So instead of going out, they sat at his house and talked.

The two began dating off and on, but Melinda was strict about the rules of their relationship: she refused to go to Bill on anything work related, and she wanted no public exposure at all (a bit of a challenge, given Bill's celebrity status after Microsoft's **IPO** left him a billionaire). Melinda remembers, "It reached the point that Bill would say to me, 'You never tell me what you're doing [at work].'"[10]

Melinda's rules worked, though. Bill requested that the media not disclose Melinda's name, and they respected the mogul's request. Her career was not affected by her status as the boss's girlfriend. In fact, when the two wed years later, many people wondered, "Bill Gates is marrying *who*?" So under wraps was the relationship that even a 1993 biography of Bill Gates only referred to her in passing—and by this time, they had been dating off and on for six years!

Things got much more serious as Bill approached his fortieth birthday and saw his mother stricken with terminal breast cancer. Bill began to get much more serious about Melinda and their future together. In Melinda, Bill saw similarities to his mother, who had been involved in philanthropy. Melinda had a similar spirit of giving back.

For a time, Melinda worried whether she should marry Bill. She saw his fame and fortune as depriving him of a normal life and privacy, and she wasn't sure she wanted any part of that. Melinda was notoriously private, so for her the money was more of a drawback than a benefit. She lived in a secluded house in Leschi, Washington (a neighborhood in Seattle), and neighbors reported that although she was always pleasant, she kept to herself and didn't have much company.

The pair's goals seemed as if they might be at odds, too: Bill was a go-getter capitalist who wanted to conquer the world (metaphorically), and Melinda wasn't sure those characteristics would be well suited to him eventually being a father.

But in 1993, the man who Melinda feared lacked spontaneity managed to surprise her when he orchestrated a surprise trip to Omaha to visit billionaire Warren Buffett, a friend. Buffett's company, Berkshire Hathaway, owned a jewelry emporium in the city (among *many* other businesses), where Bill took Melinda to pick out an engagement ring. Melinda chose a diamond ring—though far smaller than the one Buffett suggested. Money was obviously of little object, but practical Melinda was never one for flaunting wealth.

Late in 1993, Melinda had a bridal shower at which her future mother-in-law, Mary, read a letter she had written to the bride-to-be. It essentially said, "From those to whom much is given, much is expected."[11] That letter was a catalyst for Bill (known up to that point for being rather **miserly**) and Melinda to shift their focus to charitable giving. Even before they got married, they had started their first charity, the William H. Gates III Foundation, which Bill's father ran.

The two married on January 1, 1994, in front of 130 guests in Lanai City, Hawaii, after dating for more

Bill and Melinda Gates at a reception at their home a week after
their wedding

than six years. Typical of their courtship, the wedding
was shrouded in secrecy. To keep the media at bay, Bill
booked all 250 rooms at the Manele Bay Hotel, where
the wedding party was staying, and it's reported that
he hired all the helicopters on Maui so that the media
wouldn't be able to fly over and get pictures.

It has turned out to be a strong marriage, enduring
two decades and counting, and producing three children.
Friends of the couple say that Melinda brings out the fun
side in Gates and that she has helped him become more
open, patient, and compassionate. They also say that she
isn't afraid to stand up to the man who intimidates many.

A friend of the couple, William Ballantine, says, "She's very much rooted in who she is … She's not afraid of correcting Bill or saying here's another way to think of things."[12] She brings balance to the notoriously business-driven Bill. After five years of marriage, Bill commented to *Newsweek*, "I have a much more balanced life. I think I'm wiser about a lot of things."[13]

Bill and Melinda's partnership as the two halves of the Bill and Melinda Gates Foundation grew as their relationship grew and began to take formal shape around the time they married.

## Meanwhile, Back at Microsoft

By 1994, Bill and Melinda Gates were married and starting to form their early charitable foundations. But from 1987, when she started at Microsoft, to 1994, Melinda was climbing the corporate ladder at Microsoft, making a respectable name for herself that had everything to do with her qualifications and nothing to do with her relationship with Bill. In fact, her coworker Ruth Warren felt that Melinda's personal connection to Bill may have actually *slowed* her climb at Microsoft because people didn't necessarily trust that she wouldn't bring issues to Bill.

Melinda was scrupulous about keeping the two parts of her life separate, and Ruth Warren credits Melinda for successfully separating the two aspects of her life at staff meetings where people would joke about Bill. According to Warren, "People would tell a joke about Bill being a nerd, or some mean story, and [Melinda would] just hold her peace and get the meeting back on track. This was the man she was dating. I would have gone crazy, but she was professional, and I really respect her for that."[14]

When she started at Microsoft as a marketing manager, Melinda had two goals: She wanted to run a marathon, and she wanted to be given responsibility for Microsoft Word for **MS-DOS**, a precursor to Microsoft Word for Windows, which made Microsoft a household name even among people who hadn't a clue what MS-DOS was. She achieved both goals.

She went on to work on Word for Windows, as well as Works (another word-processing program), Publisher (a desktop publishing application), and Money (financial planning and tracking software). As a general manager of information products, overseeing up to three hundred employees, she also worked on Expedia, a well-known travel-planning website, an interactive movie guide called Cinemania, and a digital encyclopedia known as Encarta. In short, she worked on some of Microsoft's biggest products. But her track record at the company wasn't flawless. Melinda was a marketing manager on Bob, which was a dismal failure.

Melinda ultimately worked for Microsoft for nine years, resigning in 1996 when she and Bill had their first child, so that she could be at home with their children and focus her professional time on her and her husband's philanthropic efforts. Had Melinda chosen to stay at Microsoft, her former boss Patty Stonesifer, who is now CEO of the Gates Foundation, says Melinda would certainly have been on the executive team.

Melinda Gates barely spoke a public word for the first fourteen years of her and Bill's marriage, but she worked quietly behind the scenes on their charitable foundations while raising their children. When their youngest child started school, Melinda stepped out of the shadows and became an advocate and a public face of the Bill and Melinda Gates Foundation.

# *Microsoft Misses: Who Is Bob?*

Bob wasn't actually a "who," it was a "what." Back in the early days of personal computing, some of the general public found themselves intimidated by using computers. And for good reason: early operating systems such as MS-DOS made perfect sense to "computer geeks" like Bill and Melinda Gates and other tech giants, but they weren't exactly intuitive for people who had never really worked on computers before.

Early versions of Windows featuring the Program Manager were intended to be simple and user friendly. Programs were arranged visually in the Program Manager, easy to find and navigate! But some users were still intimidated. This was a generation of people who hadn't grown up with computers; they had grown up with typewriters. This was all new territory for many people.

Enter Bob. Bob was intended to take the user-friendly visual aspects of Windows to a new level. It was cutesy and resembled a cartoon world. Screens depicted a house, and users could click on various objects in the house to access a particular program. Want to access the word processor? Click on the pen and paper! Want to work on your finances? Click on the checkbook.

The house in Bob even came with a pet dog named Rover, who would offer helpful suggestions to users in text printed in speech balloons. Many users found Rover more annoying than helpful, though. And unfortunately, Microsoft didn't learn from their mistake on that one. A successor to Rover was the widely hated Clippy, another

Melinda Gates shows a copy of Microsoft Bob in 1995.

interactive "assistant" similar to Rover that Microsoft included in several versions of Microsoft Office starting with Office 97. Clippy actually achieved somewhat of a cult status, though. He was widely mocked in popular culture, and computer users from that era reminisce about the obnoxious Clippy, who would not-so-helpfully interrupt a user's work to announce things like, "It looks like you're writing a letter. Would you like help?" Many a user bellowed, "NO! Just let me write the letter!" at the screen before dismissing Clippy.

All of this is to say that even a giant like Microsoft and a smart and astute marketing manager like Melinda Gates can slip up every now and then.

# CHAPTER THREE

# *Stepping Out of the Shadows*

**D**espite Melinda's concerns that Bill's go-getter business attitude might not align well with family life, the two did start a family not long after their 1994 marriage. In 1996, they welcomed daughter Jennifer Katharine Gates. Three years later, they welcomed son Rory John Gates. And three years after that, in 2002, daughter Phoebe Adele Gates joined the family.

Melinda resigned from Microsoft in 1996 for two reasons. First, she wanted to be at home with her

Melinda Gates, circa 1995

Bill and Melinda Gates at the 2008 Olympics in Beijing

daughter. And second, she wanted to devote what working time she *did* have to her philanthropy work.

Fiercely protective of her privacy and her children's privacy, Melinda was virtually invisible to the press and general public for about fourteen years. But she was far from hiding. She was an active participant at her children's school and a hands-on parent to all three of her children. She simply guarded her privacy and that of her children by remaining invisible to the press. Her first-ever profile was for *Fortune* magazine in 2008—more than twenty years after she met and started dating one of the world's richest men.

So what *was* family life like for Melinda and Bill? It started out a bit rocky on the housing end of things. Melinda had been living quietly in a very private house. Meanwhile, Bill was building his dream house in Medina, Washington, on the shores of Lake Washington. It was basically a 66,000-square-foot (6,132 sq m) geek's paradise, with every technology available (and then some!), garages to house twenty-three cars, a 2,500-square-foot (232 sq m) gym, twenty-four bathrooms, a trampoline room, a 60-foot (18 m) indoor pool with an underwater sound system, a theater room, heated driveways, and more. The house's current value is reported to be around $123 million!

But Melinda was aghast at the house, which to her didn't feel like a family home. She ended up hiring an architect to redesign the partially built house to incorporate pieces that were important to her, such as more intimate spaces in the vast mansion, an office for her, and staff quarters.

In an effort to give their children a more normal upbringing, once the house was finished Melinda insisted that all hired help (except security people) be dismissed on weekends. She conceded to a babysitter on weekends if she and Bill are going out, but the rest of the help is off on weekends. She instituted family swimming night on Wednesdays and family movie night on Fridays. Bono, the front man for U2 who is a friend of the family, describes the house as having "a stillness to it. It's got a sort of Zen-like quality. Melinda has created that."[1]

## *No Silver Spoon*

Bill and Melinda Gates's children, Jennifer, Rory, and Phoebe, may come from an extraordinarily wealthy family, but their parents are committed to ensuring that they aren't handed everything on a silver platter. Recent reports put the Gates family's worth somewhere between $80 and $90 billion (yes, that's *billion*), but Bill and Melinda have reportedly decided to leave their children $10 million each when they die; the rest they intend to give to charity.

While $10 million is certainly not small change, it's a small drop in a very large financial bucket. Why have they decided not to leave more of their fortune to their children? First, they are dedicated to seeing their money go to helping people globally. Second, they, like a growing number of ultra-rich parents, recognize that they do their children no favors if they simply hand them a vast fortune. Their friend Warren Buffett decided to do similarly. He created a $2 billion foundation for each of this three kids and told *Fortune* magazine that he feels that the right amount to leave one's children is "enough money so that they would feel they could do anything, but not so much that they could do nothing."[2]

Musician Sting made the same decision and told the *Daily Mail*, "I certainly don't want to leave [my children] trust funds that are albatrosses round their necks. They have to work."[3] Late actor Philip Seymour Hoffman made a similar decision when creating his will, citing that he didn't want his cihildren to be "trust-fund kids." So did designer Gloria Vanderbilt, who inherited a fortune from her father and then grew it exponentially through her own business—her son won't get a penny. (Not that he has to worry—Gloria Vanderbilt's son is successful newsman Anderson Cooper.)

As for Bill and Melinda Gates, they decline to specify the exact amount each of their children will inherit, but sources say it is $10 million. Bill simply says, "It will be a miniscule portion of my wealth. It will mean they have to find their own way. They will be given an unbelievable education and that will all be paid for. And certainly anything related to health issues we will take care of. But in terms of their income, they will have to pick a job they like and go to work. They are normal kids now. They do chores, they get pocket money."[4]

The Gates family home on the shore of Lake Washington

Although Melinda hated the house at first, it has grown on her. However, she says, "I still wouldn't build it. But I like it."[5]

## Stepping Into the Spotlight

So what caused Melinda to finally step out into the public eye, at forty-three years old, after a lifetime spent protecting her privacy? Multiple factors, really.

Melinda says she would have preferred to stay out of the public eye forever. In reality, however, she explains, "I had always thought that when my youngest child started full-day school I'd step up."[6] It is just the reality of being at the head of the world's largest philanthropic organization.

But there's another piece to the puzzle: a mother's desire to be a good role model for her children. Melinda's oldest daughter, Jennifer, was twelve years old at the time, and Melinda was starting to think about her daughter's future. "I really want her to have a voice, whatever she chooses to do. I need to role-model that for her."[7]

There was yet another piece of the equation, too: Melinda's recognition that women who don't speak out rarely make history—and she was determined to make change on a level that would impact history. "As I thought about strong women of history, I realized that they stepped out in some way,"[8] Melinda says. It was time for Melinda to follow in those footsteps and step out.

Although she had worked behind the scenes on the foundation for years, her first major public recognition for her work came in 2005, when she was named *Time* magazine's person of the year, along with her husband and the musician Bono. The recognition came after the couple pledged $750 million to promote vaccination for children who don't have access to the vaccines they need. *Time* pointed out that Bill and Melinda Gates spent 2005 "giving more money away faster than anyone ever has."[9] Just like that, the famously private Melinda Gates had her face on the cover of a magazine and became a household name. It became apparent to many

*Time* magazine's 2005 Persons of the Year

what she had spent the past years working on, while raising her children.

## History of the Bill and Melinda Gates Foundation

Although Melinda officially entered into the public eye around 2005, she had been working behind the scenes for the Bill and Melinda Gates Foundation for some time.

It was actually around the time that Bill and Melinda got engaged, in 1993, that the two began thinking about how to use Bill's massive fortune for good and start donating to causes they felt were worthwhile. At Melinda's wedding shower, a letter written by Bill's terminally ill mother, encouraging them to give back, prompted them to take action. Along with Bill's father, they set up the William H. Gates III Foundation.

It should be noted, too, that there was a tax reason for setting up a foundation. Bill's vast fortune and income were subject to hefty taxes, and setting up a charitable foundation is one way that the mega-rich can soften the blow of taxes. Still, there was **altruism** behind the foundation, too. It made wise tax sense for Bill Gates to start a foundation, but as long as he was doing so, he and Melinda could at least use the money to promote causes they felt were important to humanity.

One of their first charitable acts was to donate laptops to schools for use in classrooms. Given that Bill was a software mogul, some people thought this was self-serving—get Microsoft in the schools, and more people will buy the products at home—but it was actually part of a larger goal. Melinda was volunteering in several Seattle schools, and she felt that bridging the technology gap in high schools could help with education reform. Technology was becoming a necessity in the world, and students in less advantaged schools didn't have access to computers, which put them at a disadvantage compared to their more privileged peers. Putting laptops in classrooms was meant to level the playing field and change the relationship between technology and education.

Shortly after Bill and Melinda's 1994 wedding, Melinda set her sights on global health reform after reading a news story about children in developing countries dying of illnesses that either rarely show up or are treatable in the United States. For example, rotavirus is a fairly common stomach virus that almost all children get by the time they reach five years old. In the United States, it results in more than four hundred thousand doctor visits each year but only twenty to sixty deaths. Worldwide, however, it is responsible for hundreds of thousands of deaths annually. Why the **disparity**? Because health conditions and medical treatment in many developing countries are far inferior to those in the United States, so what is a simple (albeit unpleasant) virus for a child in the United States can be deadly for a child in a developing nation.

Statistics like these troubled Melinda tremendously, and she brought her concerns to Bill, who agreed that their foundation ought to tackle global health issues. In typical Bill Gates fashion, he approached the problem systematically, reading the 344-page World Bank 1993 Development Report, which offered a cost analysis of the diseases. But Melinda is a more hands-on, experiential learner, so while she reads voraciously and studies up on the problems the foundation is tackling, she is at her best when working one-on-one with the people their work benefits.

Charlotte Guyman, a retired Microsoft executive and friend of the family, went to Calcutta, India, with Melinda in 2004, while Melinda was working for the foundation but hadn't yet stepped into the public eye. Guyman remembers a visit to Mother Teresa's Home for the Dying, where Melinda spent time with a woman dying from **AIDS** and tuberculosis. The woman was sitting like a zombie, not responding to anyone. Guyman recalls:

> *Melinda walks in, pauses, and goes right over to this young woman. She pulls up a chair, puts the woman's hand in her hands. The woman won't look at her. Then Melinda says, "You have AIDS. It's not your fault." She says it again: "It's not your fault." Tears stream down the woman's face, and she looks at Melinda. Melinda sat with her. It seemed like forever.*[10]

Melinda brings to the Gates Foundation the personal element that some people think Bill is missing. He isn't known for being antisocial by any means, but he is so focused on business and technology that his thinking tends to be more focused on the numbers end of things, where Melinda is strongly focused on the human aspect. In a 2015 interview, Melinda told the George H. Heyman, Jr. Center for Philanthropy and Fundraising at New York University:

> *Spending time with families is the most important thing I do, period. It keeps me motivated, because their courage in the face of great odds always reminds me why I'm doing this work in the first place. It also teaches me more than any book or conference can. When I talk with women and girls about their day-to-day lives, problems and solutions become very concrete instead of abstract.* [11]

On the other hand, Warren Buffett says of his friends, "Bill is an awkward guy. He's lopsided, but less lopsided since he's with Melinda." [12] And so, Bill works to his strengths, exploring the technological and scientific ends of their work, while Melinda plays to her strengths and works on the personal and cultural aspects of their work. Bill freely admits his focus on the more technical end of things. In a 2011 interview, he addressed the "geek" label that follows him around, saying, "Hey, if being a geek means you're willing to take a 400-page book on vaccines and where they work and where they don't, and you go off and study that and you use that to challenge people to learn more, then absolutely. I'm a geek. I plead guilty. Gladly." [13] Luckily, he has Melinda's more human-focused side to balance out his geek tendencies!

As the foundation's work has continued, Melinda and Bill have had some tremendous successes and also learned some lessons. As Melinda says, "It's always been one step forward and one step back."[14] For example, education reform didn't quite work as smoothly as Melinda had hoped. In 2008, Melinda stated, "I thought that if we got enough schools started, people would say, 'Let me build schools just like that.' Just the opposite is true. You could get 1,000 schools up and running, and the system would pull them down."[15] The couple saw lack of community engagement and appropriate leadership torpedo some of their school efforts in Seattle and in Denver. But, as they are constantly doing, they reevaluated their plan, tweaked the problem areas, and continued with their mission.

The foundation started relatively modestly, but it grew significantly when the couple's friend Warren Buffett decided to give a sizable chunk of money to the foundation in the form of annual contributions of shares of his Berkshire Hathaway **Class B** stock, to total ten million shares over the years. The first installment was five hundred thousand shares and was valued at $1.5 billion—quite a significant sum!

What caused Buffett to give the foundation so much money? After the death of his beloved wife, Susie, he decided to begin giving away his fortune. He chose to do this through the Gates Foundation because he says Bill and Melinda are experts in philanthropy, where he is not.

Melinda Gates and Warren Buffett at a 2011 press conference in New Delhi, India

He sees himself and Susie in Bill and Melinda—much like Buffett describes Bill as "lopsided," he sees himself the same way and says, "Susie made me less lopsided, too."[16] Buffett admits that he's not entirely sure he would have given the Gates Foundation such a large donation if Melinda were not part of the foundation. He sees her as being smarter in big-picture issues than her husband, which makes her an excellent asset to the foundation.

A requirement for Buffett's annual contributions is that they have to be spent in full the following year, plus an additional 5 percent of the foundation's net assets;

the money cannot simply sit in the foundation account indefinitely. That works, since the foundation has plenty of areas in which to disburse funds. Buffett also specified that the contributions will continue (until the ten million shares are all disbursed) as long as Bill or Melinda Gates is active in the foundation.

Although the foundation started as the William H. Gates III Foundation, by 2000 Bill and Melinda had combined the foundation with two other charitable organizations: the Gates Library Foundation and the Gates Learning Foundation. The combined foundation was relaunched as the Bill and Melinda Gates Foundation, which is what it's still known as today— or, less formally, the Gates Foundation. Although the foundation has several partnerships and endowments, Bill and Melinda Gates themselves have contributed more than $28 billion of their fortune to the foundation.

Melinda Gates was always part of the foundation behind the scenes, but ever since she was named one of 2005's Persons of the Year and officially stepped into the public eye around 2008, she has become, perhaps even more so than her husband, *the* face of the foundation.

## CHAPTER FOUR

# Contributions of the Gates Foundation

N o doubt Melinda Gates has made *many* contributions to the world. As a mother, she is raising three children with the values and spirit that should inspire them to continue the positive work she has done globally. To get a **quantitative** view of what Melinda Gates has contributed to the world, one need look no further than the work of the Bill and Melinda Gates Foundation, which she has dedicated the last

Melinda Gates meets with sick children in Benin, Africa, in 2010.

couple of decades of her life to and intends to continue dedicating her life to.

## The Goal Areas of the Gates Foundation

The Gates Foundation is ambitious and wide reaching in its goals, but Melinda and Bill recognize that throwing money at anything and everything would not be productive. In determining where to spend the foundation's funds, Melinda says she and Bill ask themselves two questions:

• Which problems affect the most people?
• Which problems have been neglected in the past?

Melinda says, "We literally go down the chart of the greatest inequities and give where we can effect the greatest change."[1] As a result, they tend to skip large, well-established charities such as the American Cancer Society (despite its focus on health, which is one of the areas of focus for the foundation) and instead choose to direct funds to entities working to eradicate diseases like malaria, tuberculosis, and AIDS in developing nations.

Vaccines are a big focus for Bill, and while Melinda supports his passion, she tends to dig a little deeper into root causes for the diseases and how they can take immediate steps to try to help **eradicate** them. For example, while Bill is interested in the development of a malaria vaccine (and indeed, Melinda supports that very long-term goal), Melinda focuses on ways to more immediately reduce the threat of malaria, such as funding bed nets treated with insecticide to reduce the numbers of people getting bitten by malaria-carrying mosquitos while they sleep.

The Rockefeller Foundation, another giant in the philanthropy world, formed an alliance with the Gates Foundation in 2006, and Rockefeller Foundation president Judith Rodin says, "Melinda is a total-systems thinker. She and Bill dive into issues. They care deeply, deeply, deeply about making a difference, but they don't get starry-eyed. They demand impact."[2]

Indeed, impact is what Melinda and Bill Gates are all about. While Bill sometimes focuses on the longer-term goals, Melinda focuses on immediate impact.

To maximize the Gates Foundation's impact, Bill and Melinda have narrowed their focus into four main areas:

- Global health
- Global development
- Global policy and advocacy
- US program

Each of the four areas has a number of focuses, and all of them emphasize collaborative, innovative solutions that yield results.

## Global Health Division

Broadly speaking, the foundation's Global Health Division seeks to use advances in science and technology to help save lives in developing nations. Under the umbrella of this division, there are numerous work areas. The foundation funds research and opportunities in:

- Enteric and diarrheal disease. Their goal is to end diarrheal disease deaths in children by the year 2030. Although diarrheal disease deaths are relatively rare in the United States, it is still a pressing problem worldwide.
- HIV. **HIV** is relatively well funded in the United States, but there is still no known cure for AIDS, the syndrome caused by HIV. In some developing regions, such as sub-Saharan Africa, the rate of infection is extremely high. Globally, nearly thirty-seven million people are living with HIV, and the Gates Foundation seeks to fund the development of interventions to prevent new HIV infections and to continue that decline in the spread of HIV that has been occurring over recent years.
- Malaria. The foundation's goal is to completely eradicate malaria, which continues to cause hundreds of thousands of deaths per year, primarily among children in sub-Saharan Africa.
- Neglected tropical diseases. These are infectious diseases that run rampant in developing nations

but aren't widely seen in the United States and so do not get much funding. Thousands of people in developing nations die from these neglected tropical diseases every year, and the foundation seeks to control and eventually eradicate these illnesses.

- Pneumonia. Pneumonia claims far fewer lives now than it did two decades ago, but globally it is still the leading killer of children under the age of five. Most children in the United States who develop pneumonia are successfully treated, but that's not true in developing countries in sub-Saharan Africa and South Asia, where pneumonia claims the lives of hundreds of thousands of children every year. The Gates Foundation's goal is to reduce significantly the number of child deaths occurring each year from pneumonia.

- Tuberculosis. Like pneumonia, tuberculosis still claims *many* lives globally, even though it is successfully treatable in the United States. Worldwide, deaths due to tuberculosis have declined in the past fifteen years, and the foundation seeks to accelerate that decline.

## Global Development Division

The main goal of the Global Development Division is to help poor people in developing nations find solutions to hunger and poverty. The Global Development Division encompasses several work areas:

- Agricultural development. The foundation supports projects that help increase agricultural productivity in sustainable ways, particularly in sub-Saharan Africa and South Asia, where poverty and hunger are widespread.
- Emergency response. Although we hear a lot about some natural and widespread disasters, such as hurricanes and tornadoes that periodically devastate parts of the United States, there are frequently natural disasters, emergencies, and disease outbreaks in developing nations that do not get media attention and thus do not benefit from the relief efforts that are applied during more widely publicized disasters. The Gates Foundation seeks to improve emergency response to these ignored or unrecognized events in an effort to save lives and reduce human suffering.
- Family planning. This is a particular area of passion for Melinda, which is somewhat surprising given her Catholic upbringing. Devout Catholics do not generally support anything beyond **natural family planning** and are adamantly against contraceptive use, but Melinda parts from her religion on this topic and is a strong supporter of contraceptive use and family planning. "Condoms save lives," she says matter-of-factly.[3] In developing countries, women often don't have access to contraceptives. This leads to unwanted pregnancies, but perhaps even more pressing, it leads to a health crisis in which women seek unsafe abortions. The Gates Foundation is

committed to helping 120 million women in the poorest nations gain access to contraceptives by 2020.

- Maternal, newborn, and child health. In poor or developing nations, expectant mothers do not have access to the prenatal care and health support that would allow them to have a healthy, successful pregnancy and delivery. The Gates Foundation supports efforts to improve maternal, infant, and child health so that deaths related to pregnancy and childbirth will continue to decrease worldwide.

- Nutrition. The foundation's interest in health doesn't end with pregnancy and childbirth. They also support efforts to ensure that women and children have adequate nutrition to live healthy lives. Poor nutrition often contributes to childhood illnesses and deaths, and the foundation hopes nutritional improvements will ensure better lifelong outcomes for women and children.

- Polio and vaccine delivery. The Gates Foundation has a goal to eradicate polio worldwide. This goal has nearly been accomplished, thanks to efforts by the World Health Assembly and the Global Polio Eradication Initiative, but there are still two countries that have not eradicated polio: Pakistan and Afghanistan. A polio vaccine exists; it's simply a matter of using it to its fullest effect in those nations, which is difficult given political tensions with those countries, as well as cost. The foundation's goal is to support sustainable vaccine coverage and thus prevent more than 11 million deaths, 3.9 million disabilities, and 264 million illnesses (due to polio and other diseases for which vaccines exist) by 2020.

- Financial services for the poor. The foundation supports efforts to help people in developing nations gain access to digitally based financial tools so that they can budget for their future and achieve greater financial stability.
- Global libraries. The Gates Foundation supports efforts to improve technology access at public libraries and has a goal that by 2030, the world's 320,000 public libraries will offer internet access and support to people in developing or rural areas that currently cannot access online information.
- Water, sanitation, and hygiene. Here in the United States, access to sanitary water and bathrooms is pretty much a given, but that is not the case worldwide, where 40 percent of the world's population does not have access to adequate sanitation facilities. This in turn leads to polluted drinking water for many. The foundation supports the development of new sanitation technologies in an effort to provide universal access to sanitation services worldwide.

## Global Policy and Advocacy Division

The Global Policy and Advocacy Division builds relationships and works to promote policies that advance the foundation's work. It encompasses a couple of work areas:

- Tobacco control. Tobacco is a known contributor to poor health, and with the foundation's interest in health-related programs, it's no surprise that they support programs to decrease tobacco use, particularly in developing and middle-income nations.
- Developmental policy and finance. The Gates Foundation supports the use of research, ideas, and innovation to influence public policymaking nationally and globally.

## United States Division

The United States Division primarily works on education reform at the **K–12** and **postsecondary** levels, while also working to support families in need in Washington State. The division has three main areas of work:

- K–12 education. The foundation supports efforts to improve public schools from kindergarten to grade twelve, along with efforts to increase graduation rates and produce students who are ready for a successful college career.
- Postsecondary success. The foundation's ambitious goal is to ensure that all students who wish to pursue a quality college education at an affordable institution have that chance. Their ultimate goal is

that this education will lead to lifelong, sustaining careers for students.

- Washington State. Because the Gates Foundation started in Washington, where its founders live, and is headquartered in Seattle (one location, with several others worldwide), the foundation has chosen to devote efforts to residents of the state. They wish to create opportunities for children of needy families in the state to thrive, with support from strong schools and stable families and communities.

## Melinda's Work

The goals of the Gates Foundation, condensed into four main categories, are incredibly far reaching and ambitious. As one of the two foundation heads, Melinda has an unmistakable influence on the work the foundation does.

Bill and Melinda personally review any grant requests the foundation gets that exceed $40 million. Melinda insists they discuss the grant requests without notes because she thinks it is good discipline to have them committed to memory. Grant requests less than $40 million are generally handled by other foundation staff. The foundation receives upwards of six thousand grant requests per year, so even with the amount of personal attention Bill and Melinda give to the foundation, there's no way they could review every request.

# Who Makes the Decisions?

The Gates Foundation has a lot of money and a huge reach. So who decides where the money goes? Like almost anything in the business world, there's a process.

The first step of the process is developing a concept. The Gates Foundation employs program officers who identify opportunities aligned with the foundation's strategic priorities. They vet these potential opportunities with research partners, policymakers, and colleagues. If everyone agrees that the opportunity is a valid one that supports the foundation's goals, then the foundation officers make an internal decision about whether to proceed.

When the opportunity is given a green light, the foundation begins to refine it. This can happen in a few ways. The foundation may explore possible partnerships with other organizations with similar goals and experience, or they may directly solicit an organization that they know is well suited to work on the project. Sometimes, they also use an **RFP** (request for proposal) process to allow other organizations to state their case for working on the project.

Once this phase is complete, the foundation provides interested grant applicants with guidelines and templates so they can develop a proposal and budget. The foundation vets applicants and ensures that they are good candidates for the grant.

Finally, when a grantee or multiple grantees are chosen, the foundation continues to work with them throughout the life of the project to ensure that the goals of the project are met and that the quality of the work is up to the foundation's expectations.

While Melinda is aware of all areas of the foundation's work and what is going on in them, she has taken particular interest in certain ones. One example is the agricultural development goal of supporting a sustainable plan to help developing nations increase their agricultural productivity and thus limit widespread hunger. This was partly inspired by a trip Melinda took to Kenya in 2006. Meanwhile, the foundation's dedication to global health and increasing worldwide survival rates for diseases such as malaria and tuberculosis solidified after Melinda read a news story about children in developing nations dying of the diseases.

Melinda has worked to help her children understand the foundation's goals and the need to help those less fortunate in the world. The oldest two Gates children, Jennifer and Rory, accompanied Bill and Melinda on a 2006 trip to South Africa and witnessed firsthand the poverty at an orphanage in Cape Town.

At the time, the nuances of their work may have been slightly lost on the children. Upon seeing a documentary about polio, the children wanted to know whether Bill and Melinda had personally helped the little boy in the film, asking, "Did you help that kid? Do you know the name of that kid? Well, why not?" Melinda admitted, "We don't know that boy, but we're trying to help lots of kids like him."[4]

Melinda remains devoted to improving the educational system in the United States. The foundation supports the

Gates Millennium Scholars Program, which helps fund postsecondary studies for minority students. Melinda has commented, "Bill and I believe that education is the great equalizer."[5] Given that the Gates Foundation was founded based on the belief that all lives have equal value, it's not surprising that they would be committed to efforts to allow everyone equal access to education.

Lately, Melinda has put much energy into her goal of improving women's access to family-planning materials and contraceptives. She quickly deflects any notion of *her* doing all the work, though, saying in a 2015 interview, "The Gates Foundation has never achieved anything by itself. *Everything* we do, we do with partners ... But one area in which I think our leadership helped make a real difference is family planning."[6] Indeed, in 2012, she pledged $560 million toward improving women's access to contraceptives in developing nations. It is a surprising turn from the woman who went to Catholic school!

# CHAPTER FIVE

# Melinda Gates the Activist

**M**elinda Gates was relatively anonymous outside of the Microsoft world for a very long time. She started at the company in 1987 and began dating its cofounder shortly thereafter, and although she was reasonably well known within Microsoft, the name Melinda French wasn't really known to the outside world.

Melinda Gates was named Humanitarian of the Year in 2007 for her charitable work.

When she married Bill Gates, one of the world's richest men, years later, she *still* remained fairly anonymous. Most of the general public had no idea they'd been dating for nearly seven years by that point! While she raised their three children, she stayed out of the public eye.

That changed when the Melinda's youngest child, Phoebe, started full-time school. At that time, Melinda began to dip her toes in the world of the public view. When *Time* magazine named her (along with Bill) one of its Persons of the Year in 2005, the general public began to realize that invisible didn't mean unproductive— Melinda Gates had been quietly working on the couple's philanthropic efforts at the Bill and Melinda Gates Foundation for some years.

She began to do more public appearances in support of the Gates Foundation, although she still isn't a particularly ostentatious public figure. She's out in the public view as a quiet but strong figure—someone who knows what she's doing and is determined to make an impact with her smarts and determination.

Melinda became decidedly more visible in 2012, when she made public her determination to make improved family planning a significant part of the Gates Foundation's efforts in global development. "It would have been nice to stay as a private citizen," Melinda stated in 2012, "but part of the reason why I'm so public

Melinda Gates speaks in London at a 2012 summit on family planning, sharing the Gates Foundation's goal of dramatically improving women's access to contraceptives in impoverished nations.

is that it does take a woman to speak out about these issues … Why have women not been at the heart of the global health agenda? It's because we've not had enough women speaking out."[1]

## Family Planning in a Nutshell

Family planning can mean different things to different people. To some (generally those with certain religious beliefs), it simply means letting God decide how many children a family should have, and when they should arrive. In other words, let nature take its course.

To others, family planning can refer to natural family planning, which is a method in which women use the calendar, their own body temperatures, and certain other physical signs to predict when they're fertile each month. With this information, they can then choose to abstain from intercourse if they wish to prevent pregnancy, or they can engage in intercourse if they are actively trying to conceive a baby. Certain religions, such as Catholicism, support natural family planning but do not support any form of drug- or device-controlled family planning.

To still others, family planning means using available drugs or devices (for example, birth-control pills, **IUDs**, or condoms) to prevent pregnancy when a couple does not wish to become pregnant. Although this form of family planning is widely used and accepted in the United States, it is *not* condoned by certain religions. Globally, it is not used as often in developing nations, where women don't have access to pregnancy-preventing drugs and devices.

## The Controversy

Family planning is notoriously a hot-button topic. It borders very close to the abortion debate—in fact, it spills over into that debate sometimes. Particularly in countries like the United States, where many women have access to birth-control drugs and devices, there arises a moral question: At what point is a life considered a life?

In the United States, for example, the **morning-after pill** is legal. The pill works in a couple of ways: it delays or prevents ovulation, and it irritates the lining to the uterus so that a fertilized egg can't implant. Some people feel that prohibiting a fertilized egg from implanting is murder, plain and simple—a potential life is purposely denied. Others feel that a fertilized egg is simply a mass of cells and isn't yet a true "life." For some, even delaying or preventing ovulation is essentially killing a potential life.

IUDs work similarly in that they prevent fertilization (by delaying or preventing ovulation and by disrupting sperm from fertilizing an egg). Again, it becomes a moral decision as to whether that constitutes taking a potential life or simply disrupting cells.

Birth control pills generally work in two ways: they prevent eggs from leaving the ovaries, and they prevent sperm from reaching the egg by changing the cervical lining. Yet again, is this taking a life or simply altering nature a bit?

So the waters are murky, and the line is unclear. When a life is actually a life is determined by a person's personal and religious beliefs. Some feel each egg and sperm is a potential life, and nothing should be done to alter that. Others feel that the moment an egg is fertilized, it's a potential life, and nothing should be done to alter that. Still others feel that a life is not truly a life until a certain point in the pregnancy (which varies depending on who you ask, but for many people seems to be around the end of the first trimester of pregnancy).

That's where the controversy comes in. Certain religions have very strong views on birth control and family planning. In general, some Protestant and Anglican religious groups allow the use of birth control, as do some Muslim groups, Hindus, Sikhs, Buddhists, and certain branches of Judaism. It might surprise you to known that Mormons, famed for their large families, actually don't oppose birth control and instead leave it up to a husband and wife to decide their family planning method.

However, some devout Protestant groups, such as those who live by the Quiverfull doctrine, oppose all forms of birth control, including natural family planning. (Although they have denied they are members, perhaps the most famous faces of the Quiverfull movement are the Duggar family, made popular on TLC's show *19 Kids and Counting*.)

Roman Catholics aren't *quite* as strict about birth control as Quiverfull adherents, but their views are still quite strict. Artificial contraception, such as condoms, pills, or IUDs, is strictly forbidden, but natural family planning is generally accepted because it's seen as a form of **abstinence**, which they believe is the only form of contraception allowed by the Bible.

Herein lies the controversy for Melinda Gates's family planning efforts on behalf of the Gates

At Kisumu Provincial Hospital in Kenya, a nurse talks to women about prenatal care.

Foundation: Melinda was raised Catholic and still practices Catholicism. By supporting and promoting the use of artificial birth control, she is in direct opposition to the teachings of the Catholic Church. It caused quite a stir when the former valedictorian of her Catholic high school publicly announced her support for something so against the teachings of the church!

## The Controversy Ignites

When Melinda Gates announced her plan to provide contraceptives to millions of women in developing nations in sub-Saharan Africa and South Asia, as well as Latin America and Eastern Europe, she found herself on the receiving end of a lot of anger from Catholic bloggers, among other pro-life advocates.

In 2012, shortly after the Gates Foundation announced their intent, Judie Brown, president of the American Life League, encouraged Catholics to contact their bishops to take action against Melinda's campaign. Brown proclaimed:

> Individual Catholics have to take this on as a personal challenge to the integrity of the Church ... They have to become well-versed on the Catholic teaching regarding contraception. Then they have to share that knowledge ... [with] every bishop, pleading with them to defend the poor ... [Catholic bishops are] always telling us that they are terribly concerned about poor people, immigrants, undocumented immigrants ... Now is the time for them to step up and teach, in a unified body, that what is going to happen in the third world is totally unacceptable to Christ, it is totally unacceptable to his Church, and the victimization of poor women will be beyond the pale ... They must ... [call] on the Gates Foundation to stop this madness, and learn how to teach NFP [natural family planning], which is the proper answer to this.[2]

Brown wasn't alone in her feelings. Other Catholics also pointed out the incongruity of the fact that Melinda, a practicing Catholic who opposes abortion, is in favor of artificial birth control methods that prevent life.

They also pointed out that the Gates Foundation has provided millions of dollars to Planned Parenthood and the International Planned Parenthood Federation, two vast and well-known providers of abortion services in the United States and around the world.

The Gates Foundation's support of Planned Parenthood and the International Planned Parenthood Federation is sticky. They have indeed supported the organizations—to the tune of many millions of dollars—but they insist that they support the organizations' efforts to support maternal and baby health and family planning, *not* the abortion end of the organizations.

In fact, Melinda's decision to strongly support family planning is inextricably linked to her complicated feelings about abortion. In an article she wrote in 2014, Melinda said:

*In the United States and around the world the emotional and personal debate about abortion is threatening to get in the way of the lifesaving consensus regarding basic family planning. I understand why there is so much emotion, but conflating these issues will slow down progress for tens of millions of women. That is why when I get asked about my views on abortion, I say that, like everyone, I struggle with the issue, but I've decided not to engage on it publicly—and the Gates Foundation has decided not to fund abortion. ... I understand that the abortion debate will continue, but conflating it with the consensus on so many of the things we need to do to keep women healthy is a mistake.[3]*

A pregnant woman receives care at a prenatal health clinic in Nigeria.

Judie Brown of the American Life League disagrees, saying that birth control "represents a chemical assault on women and their preborn children" and that "it is not a panacea, it is a plague." Brown feels the answer is to teach women in developing nation's natural family planning instead. She argues, "In the same way that beginning to end worldwide starvation means teaching the poor how to farm, addressing the challenges of child-bearing and illness among impoverished women and families means teaching the poor natural methods of spacing children."[4]

What of the religious officials at Ursuline Academy, the Catholic high school where Gates was educated? Gates told *Newsweek* that the nuns at Ursuline support her work. Detractors point out that perhaps the support is linked to the fact that the Gates Foundation has awarded millions of dollars in grant funds to the school.

## Depo-Provera: The Drug of Choice

One of the big complaints that Catholics (and others opposed to artificial birth control) have with Melinda Gates's plan for the Gates Foundation to provide birth control to millions of women in developing nations is that the birth control of choice for this endeavor is Depo-Provera. Those opposed to Melinda's plan from an ethical standpoint see Depo-Provera as basically a killing agent. Depo-Provera contains the hormone progestin, and it works by both suppressing ovulation (so an egg is never released) and thickening cervical mucus (which prevents sperm from reaching an egg if one *is* released). Either way, the egg is never fertilized, as long as the contraceptive works as it is intended. (The failure rate is less than 1 percent.) Those who define life as beginning *before* fertilization see Depo-Provera as killing the potential for life.

Opponents of Gates's plan have other problems with Depo-Provera, too—namely, side effects. On the rare chance that Depo-Provera fails and a pregnancy results, the pregnancy has a high likelihood of being an **ectopic pregnancy**, which is deadly for the baby and can be life threatening for the mother. Depo-Provera is known to cause **osteoporosis**, which women are already at risk for. There is also a possible link to an increased risk for breast cancer among long-term users of Depo-Provera. Depo-Provera, which is an injection, does nothing to protect women from sexually transmitted diseases, such as HIV.

So why use Depo-Provera? Many reasons. First, it's an injection that last three months, so a woman only has to attend to it four times a year, as opposed to remembering to take a pill every day. Birth-control pills can be unreliable because women forget to take them every day, and even one missed pill can result in a pregnancy. Like birth control pills, condoms aren't terribly reliable forms of birth control. They can break, or men can refuse to use them—in fact, according to Melinda there is a stigma attached to condom use in Africa. Because HIV is widespread in Africa, if a woman asks her partner to use a condom, she is often accused of suspecting him of having HIV. Although condoms are reasonably effective (but not foolproof) at preventing pregnancy when used correctly, they're not a good option because women don't have full control over their reproductive rights—men may refuse to use them.

In addition, Depo-Provera is relatively inexpensive to provide, and the Gates Foundation is looking to provide this to well over a hundred million women. The foundation has partnered with Pfizer, the manufacturer of Depo-Provera, in its mission to provide the shot to women in developing nations.

Finally, the side effects that come along with Depo-Provera sound frightening, but in reality they are no more dangerous than the side effects associated with any other form of chemical birth control.

As much as Melinda's opponents would like to see the Gates Foundation teach natural family planning instead, the reality is that doing so wouldn't give women full control over their reproductive rights. Natural family planning isn't foolproof (conception can happen even when a woman has meticulously charted her cycles), and it doesn't have any effect when unfortunate circumstances, such as rape, occur.

## Why Family Planning Is So Important

Why take on this hot topic, this controversial stance that has earned her much criticism? For Melinda Gates, much of it boils down to a few main beliefs. First, she believes that every person should have equal opportunities. Second, she believes that allowing women to space out their children results in much better health outcomes for both mother and child.

In Melinda's view, the right to make reproductive choices with regard to family planning is one that should not be denied to women. For her, it's a matter of social justice. In a 2012 article she wrote for the *Daily Mail*, she explains:

> *This is the key point for me. Access to contraceptives is a social justice issue. Birth control gave me the power to lead the life I wanted ... Virtually all of us reading this newspaper had the opportunity to use contraceptives to determine our future. The vast majority of us did so without a second thought. There is no reason why poor women wouldn't want the same level of self-determination that we exercise as a matter of course.*[5]

The consequences of not having access to birth control reach beyond just the woman in question; they impact her children, too. In the same 2012 article, Melinda describes how one thread was constant in her many conversations with women in developing nations: the women wanted their children to have the opportunity for an education. In large families where women were not able to control their reproduction because they lacked access to birth control options, the older children often end up dropping out of school to care for their younger siblings or to go to work to help support the family. Further, in such families, the parents often can't afford to send all of their many children to school. The cycle perpetuates when the daughters in the family get pregnant early and have to leave school to raise their own children. It's a vicious cycle, and one that Melinda thinks

Melinda Gates believes access to family planning will help ensure that children have a chance to get a full education.

can be positively impacted if women were only given access to the tools to control their reproductive lives.

Allowing women to exercise their reproductive rights would also be positive from a health standpoint. Melinda points to science when she claims, "If every mother spaced her children at least two years apart, it would save the lives of two million children every year."[6] The Mayo Clinic points out that pregnancies within eighteen months of a previous pregnancy result in an increased risk for babies with a low birth weight and/or small size, as well as babies born preterm.

Further, maternal health would be positively impacted. While Depo-Provera does come with some potential side effects, the women without access to birth control in developing nations are facing other potentially harmful risks. Some resort to unsafe abortions in an attempt to control their family size, which can result in serious injury or even death. For those women who choose to carry all of their pregnancies to term, there can still be health risks. A study funded by the Economic and Social Research Council showed that women who had children less than eighteen months apart could have up to a 20 percent higher risk of early death. The Mayo Clinic states that women who get pregnant within twelve months of giving birth have a higher risk of **placental abruption** and **placenta previa**.

Melinda Gates found what has become her biggest calling: the health of women and children in the form of providing greater access to family planning tools.

## Melinda's Own Moral Struggle

While many have wondered how a practicing Catholic can push for giving artificial birth control to millions of women, the reality is that it was *not* an easy decision for Melinda. In fact, it's one she struggled over, as she admits in a 2012 article.

Melinda writes in the *Daily Mail*, "It was very hard for me to take a stand on this issue. I spent years wrestling with my feelings. Many people I love and respect … believe contraceptives are a sin. I didn't want to upset them."[7]

Beyond individual people, Melinda struggled with letting down the Catholic Church. She writes, "The Church itself means a lot to me. I attended Catholic schools. My great-aunt … was a nun. My Catholic values have so much to do with the kind of person and mother I am, and I was reluctant to stir up controversy." [8]

In the end, Melinda reconciled her concerns by recognizing that although the Catholic Church does not endorse artificial birth control, it *does* reinforce helping the poor. It is the poverty-stricken women in developing countries whom Melinda hopes to help by giving them the tools to control their family planning. Melinda says of her decision, "I am inspired by the voluminous Catholic literature on God's commitment to the poor. I received my Catholic education at Ursuline Academy, where we were taught to live out our motto, *serviam*—'I will serve.' I would not be so passionate about saving women's lives if I hadn't been steeped in teachings about social justice."[9]

## CHAPTER SIX

# *From the Shadows to the Spotlight*

**M**elinda Gates went from being virtually undetectable to being a household name seemingly overnight. In reality, she had been quietly making a change in the world through her philanthropy for years. Although the general public wasn't really aware of it, her hard work hadn't gone totally unnoticed. Over the years, Melinda has earned significant recognition and many awards.

Melinda Gates attending a town hall meeting in 2012

## Awards and Recognition

The Jefferson Awards Foundation was one of the first entities to recognize Melinda Gates's contributions. The foundation gives out a number of awards each year to celebrate individuals who have a strong positive impact on others. In 2002, Melinda, along with her husband Bill, was the recipient of the award for the Greatest Public Service Benefitting the Disadvantaged.

It was certainly an honor, though not an extremely visible one. Her profile changed in 2005, however, when Melinda was named one of *Time* magazine's Persons of the Year, along with her husband and Bono, the front man of Irish rock band U2.

The *Time* recognition helped make Melinda Gates a household name as she graced the cover alongside Bill Gates and Bono. In speaking about the recognition, *Time*'s managing editor, Jim Kelly, referred to tragedies unfolding worldwide on a daily basis but not grabbing headlines and support from major entities. He commented, "Who is proving most effective in figuring out how to eradicate those calamities? In different ways, it is Bill and Melinda Gates … and Bono."[1] At the time of the award, the Gates Foundation had reportedly saved roughly seven hundred thousand lives worldwide by supporting vaccination programs, had sponsored a major scholarship, and had given away computers to tens of thousands of libraries, all just a few years into the foundation's work!

Shortly thereafter, Melinda and Bill won another award together: the Prince of Asturias Award for International Cooperation, which is given annually to recognize people or organizations that make notable contributions in the fields of science, the humanities, and public affairs. That same month, May 2006, the five-story Melinda French Gates Ambulatory Care Building was dedicated at Seattle Children's Hospital. According to the hospital's press release to mark the occasion, "The building honors Melinda French Gates and her work to improve the lives of children locally and around the world."[2]

For their philanthropic work in the health and education fields, Melinda and Bill were awarded the Insignia of the Order of the Aztec Eagle, a prestigious Mexican award, in late 2006.

In 2009, both Melinda and Bill received honorary degrees from the University of Cambridge. It was a rather fitting recognition, since the Gates Foundation gave $210 million to set up the Gates Cambridge Trust in 2000. This trust allows graduate students from outside the United Kingdom to study at Cambridge. Just a few years later, Melinda was again recognized in the United Kingdom when she was made an honorary Dame Commander of the Order of the British Empire, in recognition of her philanthropic work and her work on international development.

Melinda received a further honorary degree from Duke University, her alma mater, which awarded her an honorary doctor of human letters in 2013, in recognition of her philanthropic work. That same year, Melinda won the Lasker-Bloomberg Public Service Award, which honors individuals or organizations who have contributed significantly to the fields of medical research, health sciences, and public health. Melinda and Bill jointly took home a Bambi Award that same year, for their work fighting extreme poverty and working to improve global public health. The Bambi Awards are prestigious German media awards designed to honor people who inspire or touch German audiences.

Melinda has been near the top of *Forbes* magazine's 100 Most Powerful Women list numerous times, coming in third in 2013, 2014, and 2015; fourth in 2012 and 2016; and sixth in 2011. Melinda also earned the title of Woman of the Year from *Glamour* magazine in 2013 for her advocacy and philanthropic work.

In 2015, both Melinda and Bill received the Padma Bhushan, the third-highest civilian honor in India, in recognition of their philanthropic work in the country.

## How Much Do They Really Give Away?

As cofounder of the Bill and Melinda Gates Foundation, how far has Melinda's reach actually extended? It's impossible to say because she and Bill work together on the foundation, along with their co-trustee Warren Buffett and a team of more than a thousand other people. A look at how far the Gates Foundation's reach has extended gives a pretty good picture of just what Melinda's impact has been, since she is a driving force in the foundation.

At most recent calculation, the Gates Foundation has an endowment of $39.6 billion. If that were $39 million, it would be impressive enough, but it's a thousand times greater than that (literally)—it's $39 billion. From the foundation's inception in 2000 until the end of 2015, the foundation has given away $36.7 billion.

How has the foundation managed to retain $39 billion if it has already given away almost that much? There's the influx of donations from people like Warren Buffett, of course. The Gates Foundation's trust also invests unused assets in an attempt to gain a strong **return on investment**. Just like any person with a substantial amount of money would invest it to make it grow, so does the foundation invest its assets to make them grow. The Gates Foundation owns shares in numerous companies, including Berkshire Hathaway (Warren Buffett's company, which they receive shares of annually), the Canadian National Railway, Walmart, Shell, McDonald's, FedEx, Coca-Cola, UPS, AutoNation, Caterpillar, and Waste Management, among others.

These investments have caused a bit of controversy, though. Some critics say that some of the companies the Gates Foundation has holdings in are actually the same companies that contribute to poverty and pollution in developing nations. In 2007, it was reported that the Gates Foundation had investments in sixty-nine companies responsible for serious pollution, as well as shares of pharmaceutical companies that had priced their drugs well above what people in developing nations could afford. It was reported that the foundation also had holdings in companies known for supporting child labor, defrauding and neglecting people in need of medical care, and forcing people to lose their homes. The *Los Angeles Times* ran a story saying that nearly $9 billion of the Gates Foundation's money was in holdings for companies with practices that did not support the foundation's goals and mission.

The foundation agreed to review its holdings and reconsider some of its investments, but it later announced it had change its position and would be maintaining the investments that gave it the greatest return on investment.

The Gates Foundation website has a searchable database containing records of all grants given away since 2009 (and some earlier). Starting in 2013, they were one of the first foundations to join the **International Aid Transparency Initiative (IATI),** which catalogues grant data for information-sharing purposes and makes the foundation's grant spending easier to access. These factors mean that the Gates Foundation is a remarkably transparent organization that allows people to see exactly where and how they are spending their endowment.

From 2009 to 2015, the organization that received the largest amount of grant money from the Gates Foundation was Global Alliance for Vaccines and Immunization (GAVI), an organization that helps bring vaccines to people in poor or developing nations. GAVI had received grant money totaling $3.15 billion as of 2015.

The World Health Organization (WHO) received the second-greatest sum from 2009 to 2015, with $1.5 billion. The WHO works on public health, including fighting **communicable** diseases such as HIV, malaria, and tuberculosis.

On a similar note, the Global Fund to Fight AIDS, Tuberculosis and Malaria received the third most grant money, with $777 million from 2009 to 2015. Fourth was Program for Appropriate Technology in Health (PATH), a Seattle-based global health organization that works on, among other issues, vaccinations, communicable diseases, and sexual and reproductive health. PATH has received $635 million as of 2015.

The United States Fund for UNICEF, which supports the United Nations Children's Fund (UNICEF), received $461. UNICEF provides assistance to mothers and children in developing nations.

Rounding out the top ten grant recipients from 2009 to 2015 are the Rotary Foundation of Rotary International, the International Bank for Reconstruction and Development, the Global Alliance for TB Drug Development, the Medicines for Malaria Venture, and PATH Vaccine Solutions.

Notice anything about these top ten recipients? Only two of the ten are *not* related to global public health. The Rotary Foundation supports Rotary International in its efforts to achieve world peace through humanitarian, educational, and cultural-exchange programs. The

International Bank for Reconstruction and Development provides loans for developing nations.

## Future Plans

Women's reproductive rights figure prominently in Melinda Gates's future plans. As she said in 2012, "This will be my life's work."[3] Despite the backlash over being a practicing Catholic endorsing artificial birth control, Melinda has persisted in her efforts, pointing out that in the United States, 82 percent of Catholics feel that contraception is morally acceptable and that women in Africa and other developing nations should have the right to make their own decision, just as women in the United States do.

There is more on Melinda Gates's future agenda than just family planning. She strongly supports the Gates Foundation's work on global health, including providing vaccines in developing nations where children are dying of diseases that can be controlled with proper vaccination.

In 2016, she challenged the world to address the unequal distribution of unpaid work, the bulk of which falls to women, particularly in developing nations. She and her husband looked to the future by addressing their 2016 annual letter to high school students, who are "the ones who will ultimately be solving these problems [of lack of time and energy]."[4]

In the letter, while Bill tackles the issue of needing to provide clean, inexpensive energy for the world's

Melinda Gates at a Copenhagen, Denmark, conference in 2016

population, Melinda focuses on addressing the issue of women taking on the bulk of unpaid labor in the world.

Melinda defines unpaid labor as cooking, cleaning, and caring for children and the elderly. She acknowledges that these tasks need to be done, even though no one is financially compensated for them. However, the vast majority of the time in much of the world's populations, women are the ones who take on these tasks.

The division of unpaid labor varies from region to region. In North America, for example, women spend an average of approximately four hours a day on unpaid work, while men spend just over two hours a day on unpaid work. But in regions like South Asia, the distribution of labor has a much larger gap: women spend an average of more than five hours a day on unpaid labor, whereas men spend less than one hour a day on it.

The problem with this distribution of labor, Melinda comments, is the **opportunity cost**. Women miss out on doing other things because they are too busy doing unpaid labor. These other things can be something like a paying job, or they can be tasks as simple and necessary as going to the doctor to take care of their health, or doing homework so they can keep up in school.

Melinda's solution to this inequitable distribution of unpaid labor is a relatively simple economic principle: recognize, reduce, and redistribute. She challenges people to recognize that unpaid work is indeed work. It's not "just staying home with the kids"; it's doing work that one isn't compensated for. She points out how wealthier countries have been able to sway the balance of this unequal division of labor by reducing the time spent on doing mundane household tasks. For example, washing machines have drastically reduced the amount of time people spend doing laundry. Finally, she challenges societies to redistribute this unpaid labor by recognizing that it doesn't need to be attended to merely based on gender roles.

Every problem posed needs a solution presented, or no change will happen. In 2016, Melinda Gates's solution to the problem of unequal distribution of unpaid work was to bring the statistics about the division of labor to high school students' attention and challenge them to address the problem. "The solution is innovation, and you can help," she states in her letter.[5] She then provides examples of ways in which innovation could help reduce the amount of time spent on these unpaid tasks.

She goes on to challenge students to address the cultural norms that have led to such tasks being labeled as "women's work." For generations, women have been the primary caretakers of the children in most societies, so any child-raising tasks have been seen as women's work. Melinda points out that when fathers are offered paid time off from work when their children are born, they are able to form a closer bond with the child and recognize the reward and value in participating in child-rearing tasks.

The Gates Foundation's work spans numerous areas and even more subareas, yet they are all inextricably linked to the statement that drives Melinda and Bill's philanthropic work: the idea that all people's lives have equal value. All of it—even the technical innovation parts—works together to promote global health and the fight against poverty so that all people can live lives with equal value.

The Gates Foundation's efforts all work together to promote lifelong health and prosperity for people in traditionally struggling nations. Providing vaccines in developing nations and working to eradicate things like enteric and tropical diseases ensures that more children will live to adulthood. Meanwhile, they aren't simply forgotten as adults. For example, ensuring that women have access to birth control for family planning purposes means that the child who lived to adulthood—thanks in part to vaccines and a lower risk of fatal diseases, perhaps—can now exercise some control over her family's health and well being by spacing out her children.

Providing better maternal and child health care ensures that those families can continue to grow and thrive.

Further, working to provide technology services in developing nations ensures that people in those areas have a better chance to make a solid living for their family. They may not have every resource available at their fingertips like prosperous families in the United States do, but they can at least access more resources than before at libraries and other facilities, which opens up their possibilities.

As much as Melinda Gates has focused on developing nations and underprivileged countries, she has not forgotten the United States. On the contrary, her foundation continues to work on providing educational opportunities for students across the United States, and especially in Washington State, where she lives. Both Melinda and Bill recognize that the students of today are the people who will carry their philanthropic work into the future. They call upon those students to take the ideas developed through the Gates Foundation and run with them, coming up with new ideas to further help ensure that all people are recognized as having lives of equal value.

It is difficult to separate Melinda Gates's reach from that of the Gates Foundation because she is so firmly entrenched in it. One thing is for certain: no major initiative of the Gates Foundation begins without Melinda's support. In fact, Melinda's passion for helping others has driven, and will continue to drive, the Gates Foundation's work.

## A Future in Politics?

Melinda Gates remains tight lipped on her politics. Although the Gates Foundation has collaborated with the Clinton Foundation on a female-centric project called No Ceilings, and Melinda launched the project along with Hillary and Chelsea Clinton on International Women's Day in 2015, Melinda hasn't issued any statement on who she supported in the 2016 presidential race. Interestingly enough, she was among the top names on a list of potential vice presidential candidates compiled by the chairman of Hillary Clinton's presidential campaign.

Madame Vice President? Not this time around, but never say never.

*New York Times* columnist Nicholas D. Kristof said of Melinda Gates:

*In her obituary—hopefully many, many decades from now—it won't say she just married a wealthy Microsoft tycoon. Rather, it will say that she and her husband changed the course of poverty around the world. And the course of global health and malnutrition. It will say that she had an impact on more lives than anyone could possibly imagine. It's an incredible legacy.*[6]

Indeed it is.

# Melinda Gates

**1994**

Marries Bill Gates. That same year, they form the William H. Gates Foundation.

**1987**

Graduates from Duke University's Fuqua School of Business with an MBA. Shortly thereafter, she is hired by Microsoft as a marketing manager and relocates to Seattle, Washington. By late in the year, she begins quietly dating Bill Gates, founder of Microsoft.

**1982**

Graduates from Ursuline Academy in Dallas and begins studying at Duke University in North Carolina.

**1999**

Gives birth to second child, Rory Gates.

Graduates with double bachelor's degrees in computer science and economics.

**1986**

Gives birth to first child, Jennifer Gates. Resigns from Microsoft to raise her and Bill Gates's children, fiercely guarding the family's privacy and staying out of the public eye.

Melinda Ann French is born in Dallas, Texas.

**August 15, 1964**

Takes her first trip to Africa with fiancé Bill Gates, which inspires her interest in global philanthropy.

**1996**

**1993**

**2012**

Publicly announces her dedication to making access to family planning a significant part of the Gates Foundation's efforts in global development—a controversial stance given her Catholic upbringing.

**2006**

Takes multiple trips to Africa, which further fuels her passion for philanthropic efforts related to global health.

**2002**

Gives birth to third child, Phoebe Gates.

**2016**

Announces plan to tackle the unequal division of unpaid labor in developing nations, an important women's rights issue.

Officially emerges into the public eye, after her youngest child is in school full time, to become an active face of the Bill and Melinda Gates Foundation.

With husband Bill, creates the Bill and Melinda Gates Foundation.

**2008**

**2000**

Is named one of *Time* magazine's Persons of the Year for her work with the Bill and Melinda Gates Foundation, despite remaining out of the public eye to raise her children.

Is named third most powerful woman in the world by *Forbes* magazine.

**2015**

**2005**

# SOURCE NOTES

## Chapter 1

1. Abigail Pesta, "Melinda Gates on Her Life with the Richest Man in the World," *Telegraph*, November 25, 2013, http://www.telegraph.co.uk/women/womens-life/10457841/Melinda-Gates-on-her-life-with-the-richest-man-in-the-world.html.

2. Tanza Loudenback, "Get to Know Melinda Gates—One Half of the Wealthiest Couple in the World," *Business Insider*, August 9, 2015, http://www.businessinsider.com/melinda-gates-bio/#the-frenches-were-intent-on-sending-all-four-of-their-children-to-college-so-melindas-father-started-a-side-business-for-rental-properties-we-would-help-him-run-the-business-and-keep-the-books-she-said-we-saw-money-coming-in-and-money-going-out-2.

3. Sally Isaacs, *Bill and Melinda Gates* (Chicago: Heinemann-Raintree, 2009), 34.

4. O. Casey Corr, "Melinda French Gates: A Microsoft Mystery—She Married High-Profile Bill Gates, but Wants Her Life Kept Private," *Seattle Times*, June 4, 1995, http://community.seattletimes.nwsource.com/archive/?date=19950604&slug=2124492.

5. Patricia Sellers, "Melinda Gates Goes Public (Fortune, 2008)," *Fortune*, March 16, 2016, http://fortune.com/2016/03/16/melinda-gates-fortune-classic.

6. Ibid.

7. "Ursuline Dedicates the French Family Science, Math, and Technology Center," Ursuline Academy of Dallas. May 7, 2010, http://www.ursulinedallas.org/podium/default.aspx?t=204&id=546696.

8. "My Giving Story: Melinda Gates." *Duke Forward*, November 20, 2015, https://dukeforward.duke.edu/news/my-giving-story-melinda-gates.

9. Corr, "Melinda French Gates: A Microsoft Mystery."

10. Cathy N. Davidson, "Melinda and Bill Gates Give $20 Million to Duke University to Launch Program Expanding Interdisciplinary Teaching and Research," Bill and Melinda Gates Foundation, September 12, 1998, http://www.gatesfoundation.org/Media-Center/Press-Releases/1998/09/Duke-University.

11. "My Giving Story: Melinda Gates."

12. Ibid.

## Chapter 2

1. Sellers, "Melinda Gates Goes Public."

2. Ibid.

3. Ibid.

4. Ibid.

5. "Some of That Magic." *Daily Celebrations*, October 28, 1999, http://www.dailycelebrations.com/102899.htm.

6. Corr, "Melinda French Gates: A Microsoft Mystery."

7. Sellers, "Melinda Gates Goes Public."

8. Ibid.

9. Julie Bort, "Melinda Gates Fell in Love With Bill Gates for His 'Brilliant Mind' and 'Huge Sense of Fun,'" *Business Insider*, November 28, 2015, http://www.businessinsider.com/why-melinda-gates-fell-in-love-with-bill-2015-11.

10. Sellers, "Melinda Gates Goes Public."

11. Ibid.

12. Corr, "Melinda French Gates: A Microsoft Mystery."

13. Steven Levy, "Behind the Gates Myth," *Newsweek*, August 29, 1999, http://www.newsweek.com/behind-gates-myth-166002.

14. Corr, "Melinda French Gates: A Microsoft Mystery."

## Chapter 3

1.  Sellers, "Melinda Gates Goes Public."

2.  Richard I. Kirkland Jr., "Should You Leave It All to the Children?" *Fortune*, September 29, 1986, http://archive.fortune.com/magazines/fortune/fortune_archive/1986/09/29/68098/index.htm.

3.  Geordie Greig, "Why My Children Will Not Be Inheriting My £180 Million Fortune: Sting Wants His Sons and Daughters to Earn Their Way (and Says He's Spending All His Money Anyway)," *Daily Mail*, June 21, 2014, http://www.dailymail.co.uk/home/event/article-2662557/Sting-I-earned-money-hard-work-You-try-singing-two-hours-getting-plane-day.html.

4.  Caroline Graham, "This Is Not the Way I'd Imagined Bill Gates: A Rare and Remarkable Interview With the World's Second Richest Man," *Daily Mail*, June 9, 2011, http://www.dailymail.co.uk/home/moslive/article-2001697/Microsofts-Bill-Gates-A-rare-remarkable-interview-worlds-second-richest-man.html.

5.  Sellers, "Melinda Gates Goes Public."

6.  Ibid.

7.  Ibid.

8.  Ibid.

9.  Scott Benjamin, "Time Names Persons of the Year," CBS News, December 18, 2005, http://www.cbsnews.com/news/time-names-persons-of-the-year.

10. Sellers, "Melinda Gates Goes Public."

11. Melinda Gates and Sara Ojjeh, "Eight Questions for Melinda Gates," *Philanthropy NYU*, June 19, 2015, http://philanthropynyu.com/polIssueStory.cfm?Doc_id=326.

12. Sellers, "Melinda Gates Goes Public."

13. Graham, "This Is Not the Way I'd Imagined Bill Gates."

14. Sellers, "Melinda Gates Goes Public."

15. Ibid.

16. Ibid.

## Chapter 4

1.  Sellers, "Melinda Gates Goes Public."

2.  Ibid.

3.  Ibid.

4.  Ibid.

5.  "Melinda Gates," Biography.com, Accessed December 16, 2016, http://www.biography.com/people/melinda-gates-507408#philanthropy.

6.  Gates and Ojjeh, "Eight Questions for Melinda Gates."

## Chapter 5

1.  Joanna Moorhead, "Melinda Gates Challenges Vatican by Vowing to Improve Contraception," *Guardian*, July 11, 2012, https://www.theguardian.com/world/2012/jul/11/melinda-gates-challenges-vatican-contraception.

2.  Matthew Cullinan Hoffman, "Judie Brown on 'Catholic' Melinda Gates' Contraception Campaign: Contact Bishops," *LifeSiteNews*, May 25, 2012, https://www.lifesitenews.com/news/judie-brown-on-catholic-melinda-gates-contraception-campaign-contact-bishop.

3.  Melinda Gates, "Reflections on My Recent Travels," *Impatient Optimists*, June 2, 2014, http://www.impatientoptimists.org/Posts/2014/06/Reflections-on-My-Trip-to-Toronto#.V__6gqOZPm0.

4.  Lisa Bourne, "Melinda Gates: 'I Have Really Gone All In on Family Planning,'" *LifeSiteNews*, June 2, 2016, https://www.

lifesitenews.com/news/melinda-gates-i-have-really-gone-all-in-on-family-planning.

5.  Melinda Gates, "Bill Gates' Catholic Wife Melinda: My Agony at Being Brought Up to Believe Contraceptives Are Sinful … but Wanting Women to Have a Choice," *Daily Mail*, July 21, 2012, http://www.dailymail.co.uk/news/article-2176945/Bill-Gates-Catholic-wife-Melinda-My-agony-brought-believe-contraceptives-sinful--wanting-women-choice.html.

6.  Ibid.

7.  Ibid.

8.  Ibid.

9.  Ibid.

## Chapter 6

1.  "TIME Names Bono, Bill and Melinda Gates Persons of the Year," CNN.com, December 15, 2005, http://www.cnn.com/2005/US/12/18/time.poy/index.html?iref=mpstoryview.

2.  "Children's Hospital Dedicates Melinda French Gates Ambulatory Care Building," Seattle Children's Hospital Research Foundation, May 1, 2006, http://www.seattlechildrens.org/media/press-release/2006/05/000796.

3.  Moorhead, "Melinda Gates Challenges Vatican by Vowing to Improve Contraception."

4.  Bill Gates and Melinda Gates, "Two Superpowers We Wish We Had," *Gates Notes*, February 22, 2016, https://www.gatesnotes.com/2016-Annual-Letter?WT.mc_id=02_22_2016_20_AL2016_MED-media_&WT.tsrc=MEDmedia.

5.  Ibid.

6.  Julia Ioffe, "Melinda Gates: The Advocate," *Glamour*, October 30, 2013, http://www.glamour.com/story/melinda-gates.

# GLOSSARY

**abstinence** Refraining from engaging in sexual intercourse.

**acerbic** Sharp or biting.

**AIDS** Acronym for acquired immune deficiency syndrome. A disease that attacks the body's immune system. There is no known cure, and people with AIDS generally die of an AIDS-related infection.

**alma mater** One's former school.

**altruism** Selfless concern for the well being of other people.

**candy striper** A teenage hospital volunteer.

**Class B** A type of share of stock that does not carry as many voting rights as a Class A share.

**Clone** A computer that simulates the operation of another computer. A clone is usually a less expensive version of a name-brand computer.

**communicable** Contagious.

**disparity** Difference.

**ectopic pregnancy** A pregnancy in which the fetus develops in the fallopian tube instead of in the uterus. It is a fatal condition for the fetus and can be life threatening for the mother.

**endowment** A donation of money or property to a nonprofit organization for the ongoing support of that organization.

**eradicate** Put an end to.

**HIV** Acronym for human immunodeficiency virus. This is the virus that causes AIDS.

**IATI** Acronym for International Aid Transparency Initiative. This initiative was designed to provide the public with information on how international charitable funds are spent.

**IPO** Acronym for initial public offering. Describes when a company's stock shares are made available for the public to buy.

**IUD** Acronym for intrauterine device. Refers to a device implanted in a woman's uterus and designed to prevent pregnancy.

**K-12** Describes the school years between kindergarten and twelfth grade.

**miserly** Cheap.

**morning-after pill** An artificial contraceptive pill that can be taken up to seventy-two hours after intercourse to prevent pregnancy.

**MS-DOS** Acronym for Microsoft disk operating system. It was the operating system Microsoft used before it created Windows.

**natural family planning** A method of birth control that does not use any artificial devices or drugs to prevent pregnancy. Rather, fertile periods are calculated using a calendar, body temperatures, and cervical mucus, and participants can then abstain from intercourse during fertile periods to attempt to prevent pregnancy.

**NGO** Acronym for nongovernmental organization. Describes a nonprofit organization made up of citizen volunteers organized on a local, national, or international level. NGOs function independently of the government.

**nonprofit** An organization that uses its revenue for its purpose or mission, rather than distributing it to shareholders. Nonprofits are generally charitable organizations and are exempt from some taxes.

**opportunity cost** The loss of benefit from an opportunity that was given up in favor of another opportunity.

**ostentatious** Flashy or showy.

**osteoporosis** A medical condition in which bones get brittle and can break more easily.

**paradigm** A typical example of something.

**placental abruption** A condition in which the placenta separates from the wall of the uterus.

**placenta previa** A condition in which placenta blocks part of the uterus, causing problems in development for the fetus.

**postsecondary** Education after high school.

**quantitative** Measured by quantity (amount), rather than quality.

**return on investment** The benefit an investor receives from an investment made.

**RFP** Acronym for request for proposals. Organizations may send out an RFP to solicit potential vendors when they are budgeting out a project.

**STEM** Acronym for science, technology, engineering, and mathematics. These subjects have become known as STEM subjects.

# FURTHER INFORMATION

## Books

Hope Through Healing Hands, compiler. *The Mother and Child Project: Raising Our Voices for Health and Hope*. Grand Rapids, MI: Zondervan, 2015.

Lewis, Barbara A. *The Teen Guide to Global Action: How to Connect with Others (Near and Far) to Create Social Change*. Minneapolis, MN: Free Spirit Publishing, 2007.

Singer, Peter. *Famine, Affluence, and Mortality*. Oxford, UK: Oxford University Press, 2015.

## Websites

### Bill and Melinda Gates Foundation
http://www.gatesfoundation.org

Learn more about what the Gates Foundation does and who they support at their website.

### Cross-Cultural Solutions
https://www.crossculturalsolutions.org/high-school-volunteer-abroad

Cross-Cultural Solutions is an organization that offers specialized volunteer opportunities for teens wanting to help out in other countries.

**Global Vision International**
http://www.gviusa.com/volunteer-options/under-18

GVI offers international volunteer opportunities specifically for teens.

**Humanitarian Relief Organizations**
http://www.cfr.org/nonstate-actors-and-nongovernmental-organizations/humanitarian-relief-organizations/p9007

This page features a comprehensive list of humanitarian relief organizations that provide assistance in areas of need such as the ones the Gates Foundation works in.

**United Planet**
http://www.unitedplanet.org/teen-volunteer-abroad

United Planet is a nonprofit offering volunteer abroad opportunities for teens.

## Video

**"Why Giving Away Our Wealth Has Been the Most Satisfying Thing We've Ever Done"**
https://www.youtube.com/watch?v=aSL-iIskEFU

TED Talks: Bill and Melinda Gates

# BIBLIOGRAPHY

Benjamin, Scott. "Time Names Persons of the Year." CBS News, December 18, 2005. http://www.cbsnews.com/news/time-names-persons-of-the-year.

Bort, Julie. "Melinda Gates Fell in Love with Bill Gates for His 'Brilliant Mind' and 'Huge Sense of Fun.'" *Business Insider*, November 28, 2015. http://www.businessinsider.com/why-melinda-gates-fell-in-love-with-bill-2015-11.

Bourne, Lisa. "Melinda Gates: 'I Have Really Gone All In on Family Planning." *LifeSiteNews*, June 2, 2016. https://www.lifesitenews.com/news/melinda-gates-i-have-really-gone-all-in-on-family-planning.

"Children's Hospital Dedicates Melinda French Gates Ambulatory Care Building." Seattle Children's Hospital Research Foundation, May 1, 2006. http://www.seattlechildrens.org/media/press-release/2006/05/000796.

Corr, O. Casey. "Melinda French Gates: A Microsoft Mystery—She Married High-Profile Bill Gates, but Wants Her Life Kept Private." *Seattle Times*, June 4, 1995. http://community.seattletimes.nwsource.com/archive/?date=19950604&slug=2124492.

Davidson, Cathy N. "Melinda and Bill Gates Give $20 Million to Duke University to Launch Program Expanding Interdisciplinary Teaching and Research." Bill and Melinda Gates Foundation, September 12, 1998. http://www.gatesfoundation.org/Media-Center/Press-Releases/1998/09/Duke-University.

"Degrees in Computer and Information Sciences Conferred by Degree-Granting Institutions, by Level of Degree and Sex of Student: 1970–71 Through 2010–11." National Center for Education Statistics. Accessed December 16, 2016. https://nces.ed.gov/programs/digest/d12/tables/dt12_349.asp.

Gates, Bill, and Melinda Gates. "Two Superpowers We Wish We Had." *Gates Notes*, February 22, 2016. https://www.gatesnotes.com/2016-Annual-Letter?WT.mc_id=02_22_2016_20_AL2016_MED-media_&WT.tsrc=MEDmedia.

Gates, Melinda. "Bill Gates' Catholic Wife Melinda: My Agony at Being Brought Up to Believe Contraceptives Are Sinful … but Wanting Women to Have a Choice." *Daily Mail*, July 21, 2012. http://www.dailymail.co.uk/news/article-2176945/Bill-Gates-Catholic-wife-Melinda-My-agony-brought-believe-contraceptives-sinful--wanting-women-choice.html.

———. "Reflections on My Recent Travels." *Impatient Optimists*, June 2, 2014. http://www.impatientoptimists.org/Posts/2014/06/Reflections-on-My-Trip-to-Toronto#.V__6gqOZPm0.

Gates, Melinda, and Sara Ojjeh. "Eight Questions for Melinda Gates." *Philanthropy NYU*, June 19, 2015. http://philanthropynyu.com/polIssueStory.cfm?Doc_id=326.

"The Gender Gap: A Quantitative Description." Stanford University. Accessed December 16, 2016. https://cs.stanford.edu/people/eroberts/cs181/projects/women-in-cs/statistics.html.

Graham, Caroline. "This Is Not the Way I'd Imagined Bill Gates: A Rare and Remarkable Interview with the World's Second Richest Man." *Daily Mail*, June 9, 2011. http://www.dailymail.co.uk/home/moslive/article-2001697/Microsofts-Bill-Gates-A-rare-remarkable-interview-worlds-second-richest-man.html.

Greig, Geordie. "Why My Children Will Not Be Inheriting My £180 Million Fortune: Sting Wants His Sons and Daughters to Earn Their Way (and Says He's Spending All His Money Anyway)." *Daily Mail*, June 21, 2014. http://www.dailymail.co.uk/home/event/article-2662557/Sting-I-earned-money-hard-work-You-try-singing-two-hours-getting-plane-day.html.

Hoffman, Matthew Cullinan. "Judie Brown on 'Catholic' Melinda Gates' Contraception Campaign: Contact Bishops." *LifeSiteNews*, May 25, 2012. https://www.lifesitenews.com/news/judie-brown-on-catholic-melinda-gates-contraception-campaign-contact-bishop.

Ioffe, Julia. "Melinda Gates: The Advocate." *Glamour*, October 30, 2013. http://www.glamour.com/story/melinda-gates.

Isaacs, Sally. *Bill and Melinda Gates*. Chicago: Heinemann-Raintree, 2009.

Kirkland, Richard I., Jr. "Should You Leave It All to the Children?" *Fortune*, September 29, 1986. http://archive.fortune.com/magazines/fortune/fortune_archive/1986/09/29/68098/index.htm.

Levy, Steven. "Behind the Gates Myth." *Newsweek*, August 29, 1999. http://www.newsweek.com/behind-gates-myth-166002.

Loomis, Carol J. "How Buffett's Giveaway Will Work." *Fortune*, June 25, 2006. http://archive.fortune.com/2006/06/25/magazines/fortune/charity3.fortune/index.htm.

Loudenback, Tanza. "Get to Know Melinda Gates—One Half of the Wealthiest Couple in the World." *Business Insider*, August 9, 2015. http://www.businessinsider.com/melinda-gates-bio/#the-frenches-were-intent-on-sending-all-four-of-their-children-to-college-so-melindas-father-started-a-side-business-for-rental-properties-we-would-help-him-run-the-business-and-keep-the-books-she-said-we-saw-money-coming-in-and-money-going-out-2.

"Media Booted From Island of Bill Gates' Wedding." *Seattle Times*, January 2, 1994. http://community.seattletimes.nwsource.com/archive/?date=19940102&slug=1887661.

"Melinda Gates." Biography.com. Accessed December 16, 2016. http://www.biography.com/people/melinda-gates-507408#philanthropy.

Moorhead, Joanna. "Melinda Gates Challenges Vatican by Vowing to Improve Contraception." *Guardian*, July 11, 2012. https://www.theguardian.com/world/2012/jul/11/melinda-gates-challenges-vatican-contraception.

"My Giving Story: Melinda Gates." *DukeForward*, November 20, 2015. https://dukeforward.duke.edu/news/my-giving-story-melinda-gates.

Pesta, Abigail. "Melinda Gates on Her Life with the Richest Man in the World." *Telegraph*, November 25, 2013. http://www.telegraph.co.uk/women/womens-life/10457841/Melinda-Gates-on-her-life-with-the-richest-man-in-the-world.html.

Sellers, Patricia. "Melinda Gates Goes Public (Fortune, 2008)." *Fortune*, March 16, 2016. http://fortune.com/2016/03/16/melinda-gates-fortune-classic.

"Some of That Magic." *Daily Celebrations*, October 28, 1999. http://www.dailycelebrations.com/102899.htm.

"State of Girls and Women in STEM." National Girls Collaborative Project. Accessed December 16, 2016. https://ngcproject.org/statistics.

"TIME Names Bono, Bill and Melinda Gates Persons of the Year." CNN.com, December 15, 2005. http://www.cnn.com/2005/US/12/18/time.poy/index.html?iref=mpstoryview.

"Ursuline Dedicates the French Family Science, Math, and Technology Center." Ursuline Academy of Dallas, May 7, 2010. http://www.ursulinedallas.org/podium/default.aspx?t=204&id=546696.

Yarow, Jay. "How Apple Really Lost Its Lead in the '80s." *Business Insider*, December 9, 2012. http://www.businessinsider.com/how-apple-really-lost-its-lead-in-the-80s-2012-12.

# INDEX

Page numbers in **boldface** are illustrations. Entries in **boldface** are glossary terms.

# ABOUT THE AUTHOR

**Cathleen Small** is an author and editor who lives in the San Francisco Bay Area. She has written two dozen nonfiction books for students in fifth grade through high school, including several biographies on leading women and numerous technology titles. When she's not working, Cathleen loves to travel and spend time with her husband, two young sons, pug, and two cats.